Our Ocean World
COLOR BY NUMBERS

Our Ocean World
COLOR BY NUMBERS

David Woodroffe

SIRIUS

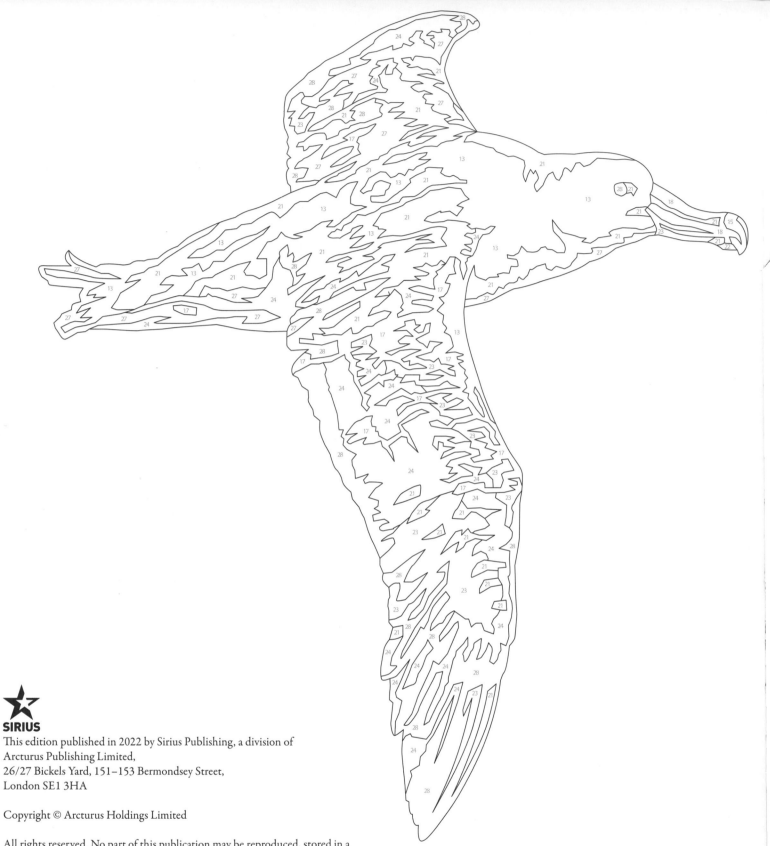

SIRIUS

This edition published in 2022 by Sirius Publishing, a division of
Arcturus Publishing Limited,
26/27 Bickels Yard, 151–153 Bermondsey Street,
London SE1 3HA

ISBN: 978-1-3988-2092-0
CH010166NT
Supplier 29, Date 1022, PI 0001809

Printed in China

Introduction

Over 70 percent of the earth's surface is covered in water—from streams and creeks to meandering rivers and mighty oceans—and it's hardly surprising that we are fascinated by the life that exists in and around the sea.

This delightful collection of images, which have been specially created, celebrates the animal life to be found both above and beneath the waves as well as the delights of actually being on water. Included here are charming scenes of exotic fish and other tropical creatures, optically puzzling patterns, beautiful birds, fully rigged sailing ships evoking the drama of centuries ago, and piratical treasure.

Whether you choose a cute dolphin, a stunning starfish, or a perky penguin, every image is guaranteed to provide hours of pleasure as you pick up your pencils or pens and add color bring them fully to life.

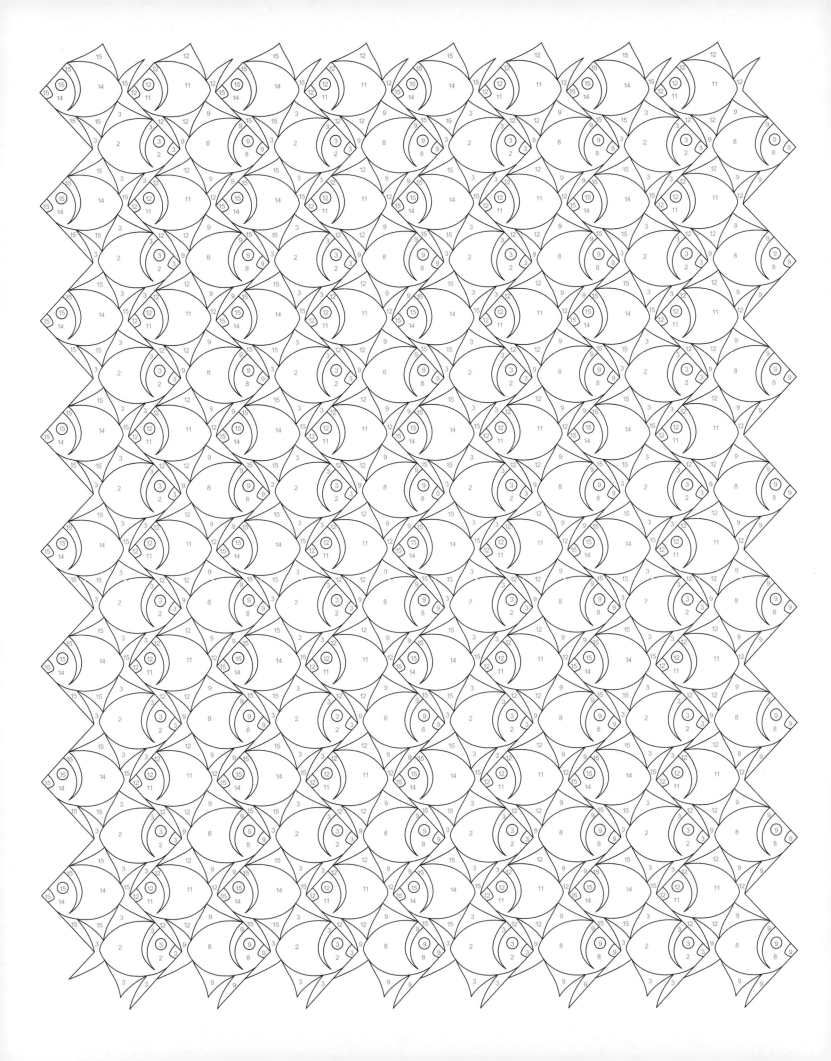

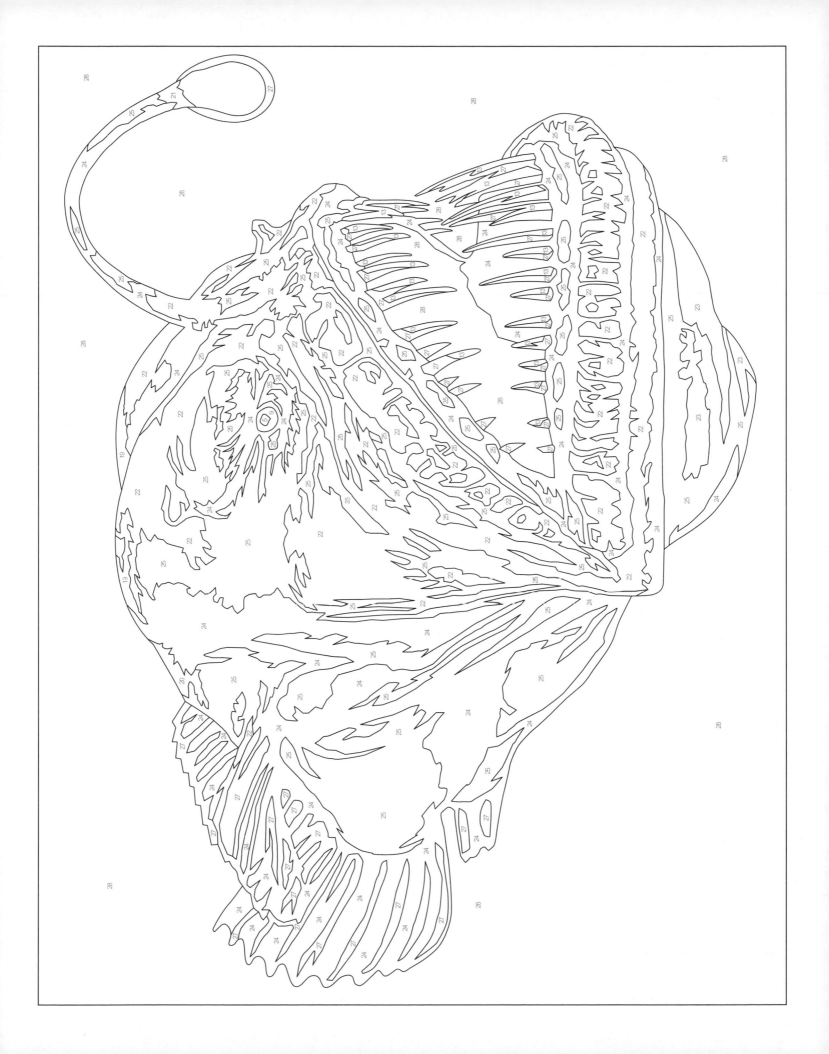

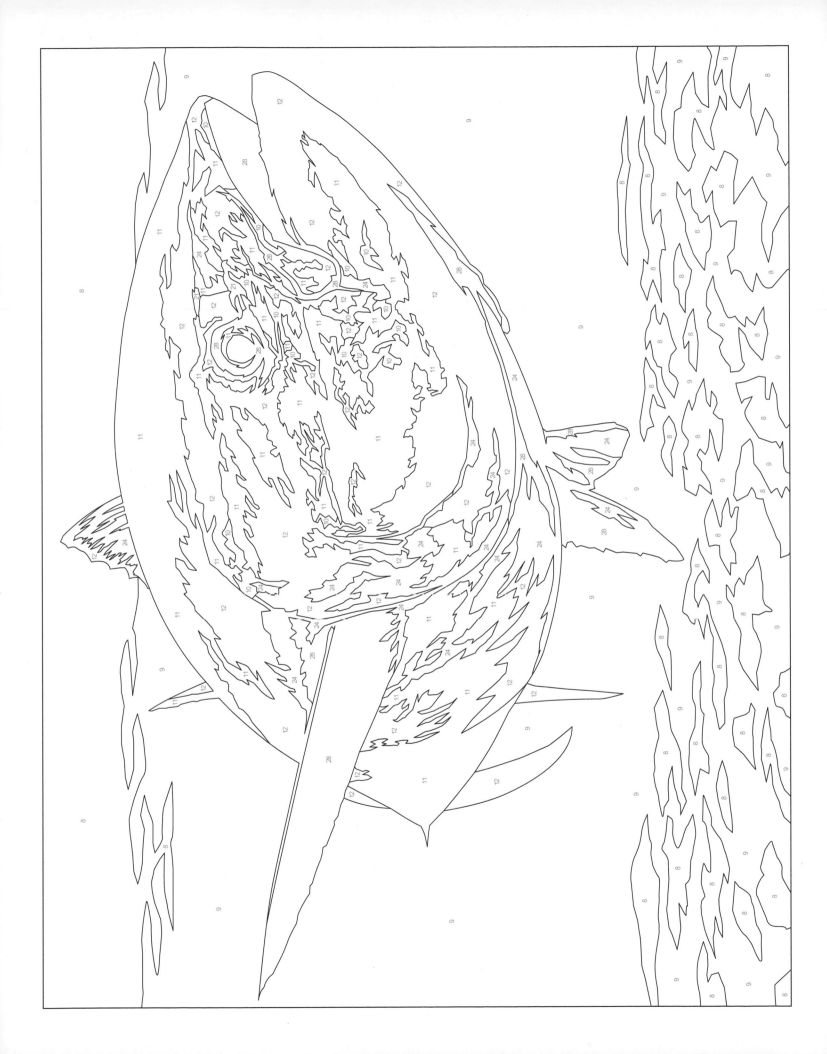

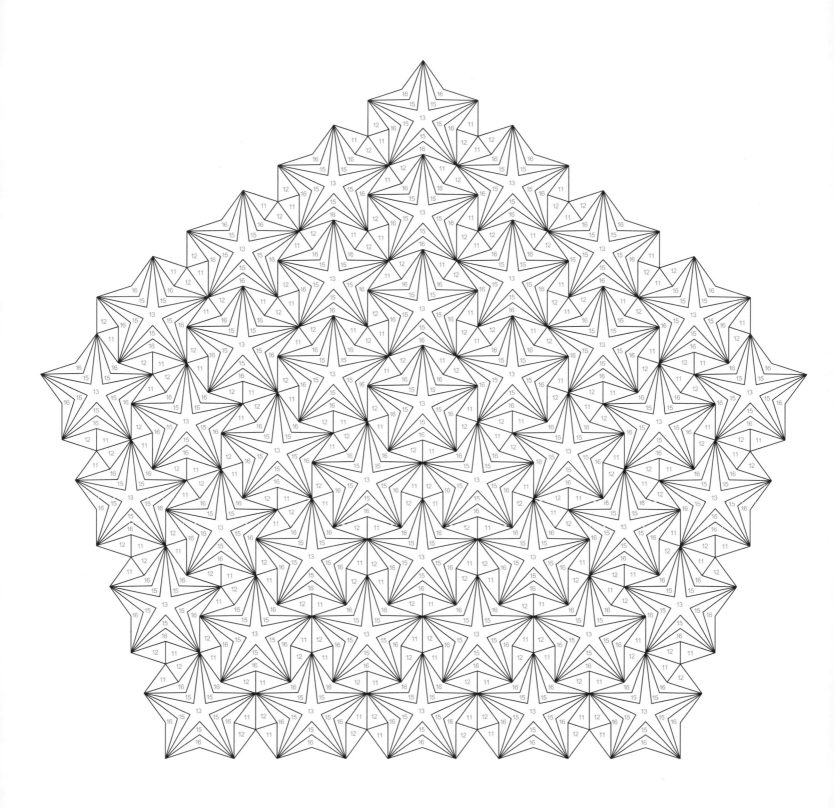

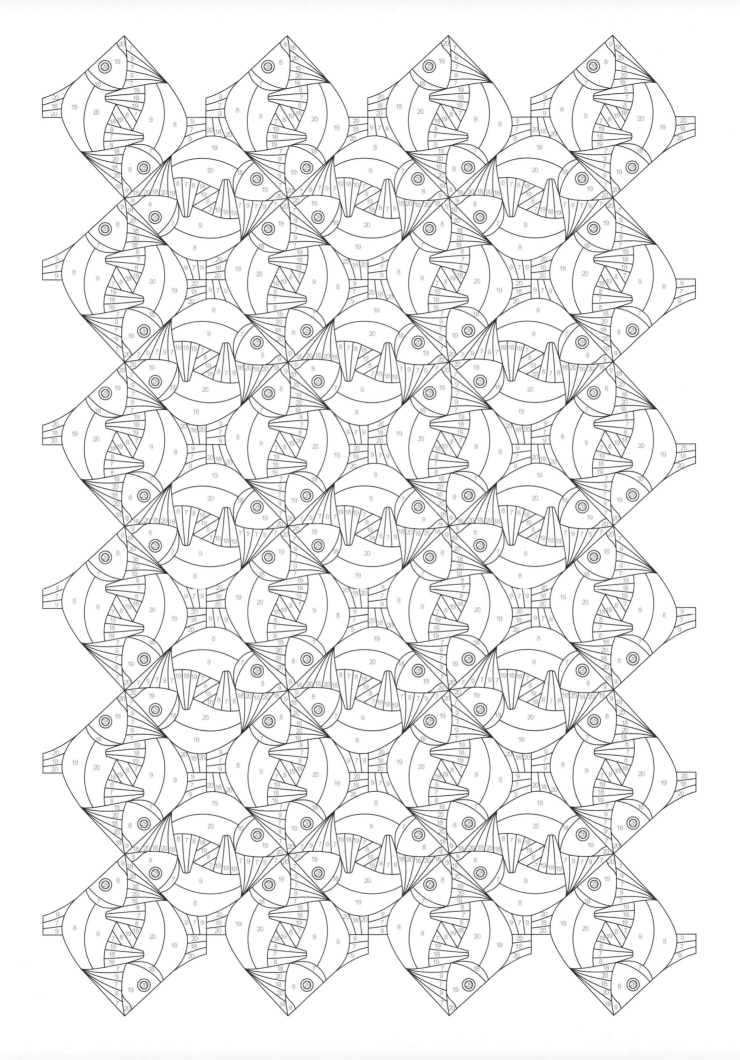

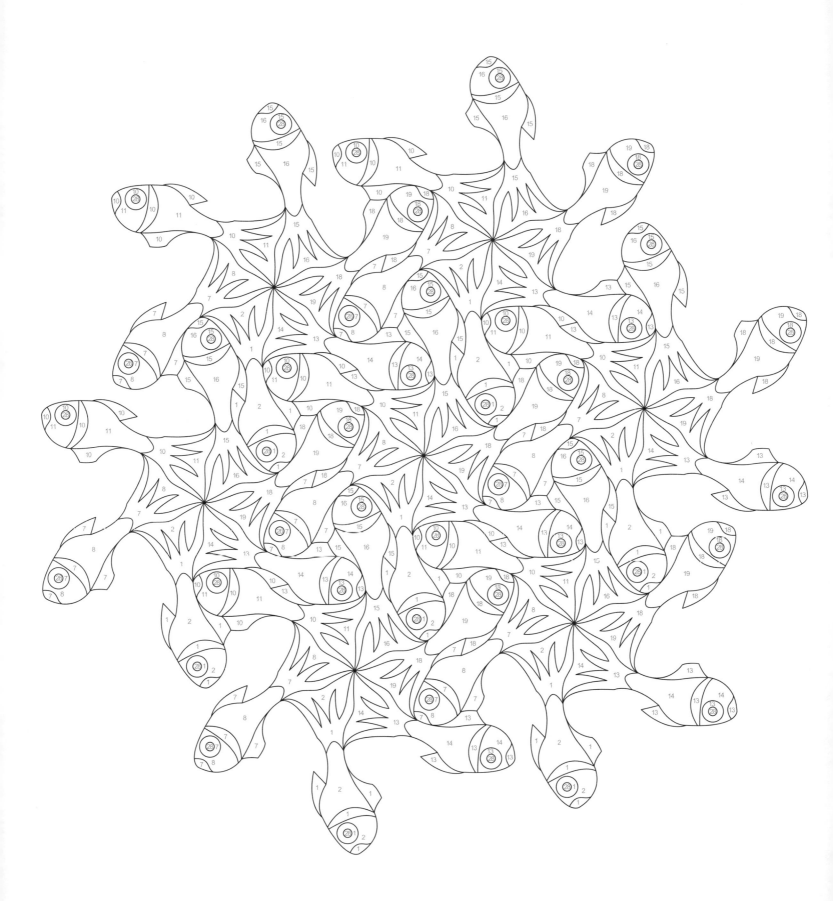

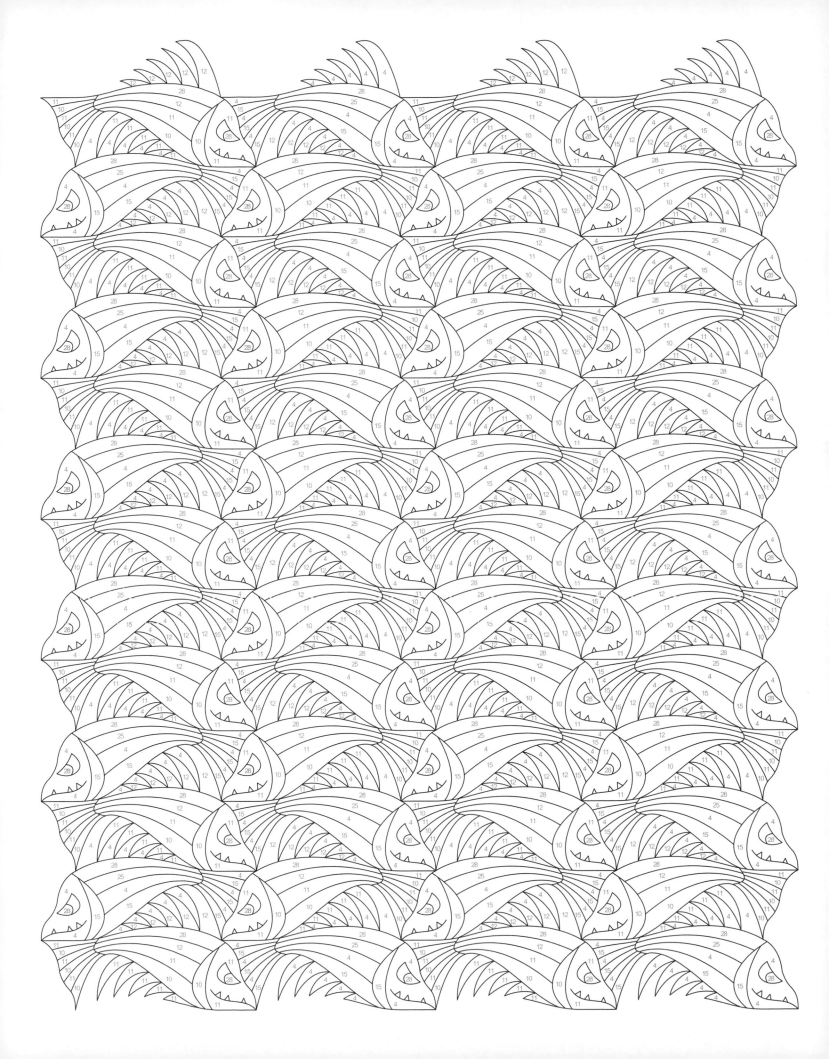